PRINTING AND PUBLISHING EVIDENCE

Thesauri for Use in

Rare Book and Special Collections Cataloguing

Prepared by the

Standards Committee

of the

Rare Books and Manuscripts Section

(ACRL/ALA)

Chicago

Association of College and Research Libraries

1986

Published by the Association of College and Research Libraries
a division of the American Library Association
50 East Huron Street
Chicago, IL 60611

ISBN 0-8389-7108-3

Printed in the United States of America.

The Library of Congress has assigned the following codes to these thesauri:

    Printing terms (signified by "A" in the thesaurus): rbpri

    Publishing terms (signified by "B" in the thesaurus): rbpub

The appropriate code must be entered in subfield ≠2 of field 755 when terms from these thesauri are used in that field. For terms that appear in both thesauri, i.e., are designated as both printing (A) and publishing (B) terms, the code should indicate the thesaurus intended. Thus the code in subfield ≠2 will correspond with the parenthetical qualifier used in subfield ≠a (<u>see</u> Introduction).

PRINTING AND PUBLISHING EVIDENCE
Thesauri for Use in Rare Book and Special Collections Cataloguing

Introduction

I. History

The Independent Research Libraries Association's <u>Proposals for establishing standards for the cataloguing of rare books and specialized research materials in machine-readable form</u> (Worcester, Mass., 1979) called for a new field to be added to machine-readable cataloguing (MARC) formats for terms indicating the physical characteristics of the material catalogued (Proposal Five), with particular reference to physical evidence for the processes of the production of printed works. In the same proposal IRLA requested that the Standards Committee of the Rare Books and Manuscripts Section of ACRL work toward developing standard terminology for use in such a field. The RBMS Standards Committee undertook the development of a thesaurus of terms, and a field for such terms (755 "Physical Characteristics Access") was authorized for all MARC formats in January 1984.

In order to expedite publication of the thesaurus, the RBMS Standards Committee decided to divide it into several separate thesauri, each treating evidence of a different aspect of book production and history.* Two of these thesauri, containing terms for evidence of both printing and publishing practices, are presented here in combined form, the many overlapping terms reflecting the close connection and shared history of the two activities. The terms in the thesauri come from drafts of the IRLA proposals, some existing lists in rare book libraries, various reference works, and comments on drafts of the list by individuals at several institutions. Major drafts of the thesauri were prepared by former RBMS Standards Committee members Alexandra Mason (printing) and Patrick Russell (publishing).

II. Purpose and Scope

Many rare book libraries, concerned with the study of the book, maintain local files recording examples of various physical characteristics of items found in their collections. These files are used to retrieve books by physical features rather than by intellectual content. Although such files are useful for selection of materials for exhibition, for class demonstration, and for cataloguing comparison, their primary use is to assist researchers interested in studying techniques and styles of book production and distribution. Reflecting for the most part local rather than standard cataloguing practices, such files have often remained available only within individual libraries. Developed specifically for use in MARC field 755, the following thesauri provide standard terms for the retrieval of physical evidence of printing and publishing practices. Such standardization is a necessity for those institutions working in the context of shared, machine-readable cataloguing but may also prove beneficial to those maintaining in-house files.

---

* The RBMS Standards Committee is presently reviewing drafts of a similar thesaurus of binding terms and another thesaurus covering genre/form and physical characteristics terms for graphic materials. Other topics for possible future thesauri include paper and papermaking, provenance, and type evidence.

III. Form

Terms in these two thesauri appear in a combined alphabetical list followed by separate hierarchical arrangements. Following ANSI standards (American National Standards Institute, American National Standard Guidelines for Thesaurus Construction and Use, New York, 1980), the terms are in plural natural language noun form whenever possible, and in direct order. Adjectives and prepositions have been avoided as far as possible. Although all terms are specific, an attempt has been made to include both genus (e.g., Facsimiles) and species (e.g., Pen facsimiles) of evidence in a number of cases.

The alphabetical list contains authorized terms and cross-references for both thesauri. Scope notes follow terms thought to be obscure or ambiguous or which are to be used in a technical sense. Each term is followed by the cross-references, if any, made to and from other terms in the thesauri. Symbols used in these references are those which ANSI prescribes:

> USE leads from unused synonyms and inverted forms of the term to the term used;
>
> UF (used for) is the reciprocal of the USE reference and accompanies the term to which the USE reference refers;
>
> BT (broader term) refers from a term for a member of a class to the term for the class;
>
> NT (narrower term) refers from a term for a class to the term for one of its members;
>
> RT (related term) is used between related terms when it seems helpful to bring associated types of evidence to the user's attention.

In the present thesauri, members of a class related to each other as narrower terms (NTs) under a common class (BT) are not related to each other as related terms (RTs). However, whenever a term for which there are narrower terms in the thesauri appears under another term as either a narrower term (NT) or a related term (RT), it is followed by the symbol ">" to indicate that it is not the narrowest concept of its class. Users should consult the entry in the alphabetical list for terms so marked to identify narrower terms.

The separate hierarchical lists (see pp. 23-28) of printing and publishing terms, furnished to provide convenient overviews, contain no cross-references, although a similar function is served by the appearance of some terms in more than one place within a hierarchy. The hierarchies contain several explanatory or gathering terms (displayed within square brackets). These terms are not authorized for use in field 755 and do not appear in the alphabetical list.

IV. Application

In a MARC record, these terms are to be entered in subfield ≠a ("access term") of field 755. Terms which do not appear in these or other thesauri approved for field 755 may not be used in this field. When used in a MARC record, a parenthetical qualifier must be added in subfield ≠a following the term. Terms preceded by "A" in the alphabetical list receive the qualifier "(Printing)"; terms preceded by "B" receive the qualifier "(Publishing)".

Either qualifier may be used with terms preceded by both "A" and "B". The qualifier will aid users who may not see or know how to interpret the coding for subfield ≠2 (see below) and also helps clarify terms which are ambiguous when taken out of context (e.g., "Crowding" or "Justification").

Any term in these thesauri may be subdivided by place (≠z), period (≠y), or other subdivision (≠x), or by any combination of these subdivisions. Each library must determine its own scheme for chronological subdivision. Indirect subdivision, as outlined in LC's Cataloging Service Bulletin 120 (1977), p. 9-11, is to be used when subdividing by place. Libraries using other subdivisions (≠x) should construct these subdivisions to conform as far as possible to LC practice as defined in publications such as Library of Congress Subject Headings: A Guide to Subdivision Practice (Washington, 1981) or Cataloging Service Bulletin.

Each field must close with a subfield ≠2 ("source of access term"). The Library of Congress has assigned the codes "rbpri" and "rbpub" to these thesauri. Fields using terms preceded by "A" in the alphabetical list should close with subfield ≠2 "rbpri"; those preceded by "B" should end with subfield ≠2 "rbpub". Codes should always correspond with the parenthetical qualifier used in subfield ≠a: "rbpri" with "(Printing)" and "rbpub" with "(Publishing)".

An example of the application of a subdivided term:

755 ⌦⌦ ≠a Signing patterns (Printing) ≠z Germany ≠y 18th
       century ≠2 rbpri

N.B.: Subfields ≠a (with qualifier) and ≠2 are mandatory, other subfields are optional.

Field 755 is repeatable; assign as many terms as appropriate and desired to retrieve types of evidence in an item. For example, a book printed on vellum containing red initials and having a gap in the signing might have three 755s: "Vellum printings", "Printing in multiple colors at separate passes", and "Signing gaps".

Use of field 755 is voluntary. Some libraries may want to use the field only for several of the terms; other libraries may prefer to use none. In the case of those terms linked by a genus-species relationship, some libraries may wish to use only the broader term; other libraries may prefer to assign only the narrower terms when appropriate, saving the broader term for items not covered by any narrower terms in the thesaurus. Some of the terms may apply to an entire edition of a particular work (e.g., Eighteenmo format), whereas other terms may apply only to a very few copies or even a single copy of a work (e.g., Type-body impressions). Libraries doing original cataloguing should describe as desired the physical characteristics of their own copies. Other libraries making later use of such cataloguing will need to evaluate the 755 entries for appropriateness to their own copies.

These terms are to be used in field 755 regardless of the appearance of the same information elsewhere in the record (such as in a subject heading or in a note), their primary purpose being to provide easy retrieval of examples of physical evidence through a single source.

The following works may prove helpful to persons needing fuller descriptions of some of the features or processes represented by terms in these thesauri:

Bowers, Fredson. _Principles of Bibliographical Description._ Princeton, N.J.: Princeton University Press, 1949.

Carter, John. _ABC for Book-Collectors._ London: Rupert Hart-Davis, 1952 (also available in many revised English and American editions).

Gaskell, Philip. _A New Introduction to Bibliography._ Oxford: Clarendon Press; New York: Oxford University Press, 1972.

McKerrow, Ronald B. _An Introduction to Bibliography for Literary Students._ Oxford: Clarendon Press, 1927, 2nd impression with corrections, 1928.

V. Revision

The RBMS Standards Committee is responsible for the maintenance and revision of these thesauri. It solicits suggestions for new terms, corrections, and alterations to terms, scope notes, and references. Any new term proposed should be accompanied by a scope note and references if appropriate. Any correspondence regarding these thesauri should be addressed to

Chair, Standards Committee
Rare Books and Manuscripts Section
ACRL/ALA
50 East Huron Street
Chicago, IL 60611

Attention: Printing and Publishing Evidence

RBMS Standards Committee Members, 1985-1986

Anna Lou Ashby
Helen S. Butz
Dianne M. Chilmonczyk
Michèle Cloonan
Alan N. Degutis
Jackie M. Dooley
Peter S. Graham
Rebecca Hayne

Paul S. Koda
Sara Shatford Layne
Hope Mayo
Elisabeth Betz Parker
Judith C. Singleton
Joe Springer
John B. Thomas III

PRINTING AND PUBLISHING EVIDENCE
Thesauri for Use in Rare Book and Special Collections Cataloguing

I: Alphabetical list

Use these terms to retrieve examples of physical evidence of production methods and of publishing/bookselling practices. Terms prefaced by letter A relate to printing house practice, those by B to publishing/bookselling practice; those which relate to both aspects are prefaced by A and B. For the companion hierarchical arrangement, see section II: Hierarchical list.

2o format
    USE Folio format

4to format
    USE Quarto format

8vo format
    USE Octavo format

12mo format
    USE Duodecimo format

16mo format
    USE Sixteenmo format

18mo format
    USE Eighteenmo format

24mo format
    USE Twenty-fourmo format

32mo format
    USE Thirty-twomo format

64mo format
    USE Sixty-fourmo format

Accidental type impressions
    USE Space impressions
        Type-body impressions

B   Advance copies
    RT Dummies
        Gratis copies
        Review copies
        Sample copies

Auction prices
    USE Second-hand prices

B Authentication
(Use for the 18th century practice of having an author sign,
stamp, or initial the title-page of a book as a protection against
counterfeit editions)
UF Author statement in manuscript
RT Copyright notices
Forgeries
Piracies

Author statement in manuscript
USE Authentication

Backing-up
USE Perfecting

A Bearer impressions
(Use for accidental impressions of roller or platen bearers)
UF Impressions, Bearer
BT Locking-up

B Binding issues
BT Issues

Blad
USE Sample copies

A B Block books
UF Xylographica

Blocks, Inverted
USE Inverted blocks

B Book designers' mock-ups
RT Dummies

B Book prices
(Use for original price only)
UF Prices of books
RT Second-hand prices

B Booksellers' labels
(Use for labels from original booksellers only, not for labels from
later resale)
UF Labels, Booksellers'

A Broadsheet format
UF Broadside format
BT Formats

Broadside format
USE Broadsheet format

Calendar styles
USE Imprint date styles

A B Cancel gatherings
    (Use for gatherings with altered text meant to replace text
    already printed, added to items after printing)
    UF Cancellans gatherings
    BT Cancellation

A B Cancel leaves
    (Use for leaves with altered text meant to replace text already
    printed, added to items after printing)
    UF Cancellans leaves
    BT Cancellation
    RT Inserted text leaves

A B Cancel slips
    UF Label cancels
       Slip cancels
    BT Cancellation

Cancellandum gatherings
    USE Cancelled gatherings

Cancellandum leaves
    USE Cancelled leaves

Cancellans gatherings
    USE Cancel gatherings

Cancellans leaves
    USE Cancel leaves

A B Cancellation
    UF Cancels
    NT Cancel gatherings
       Cancel leaves
       Cancel slips
       Cancellation marks >
       Cancelled gatherings
       Cancelled leaves
    RT Manuscript corrections
       Stamped corrections
       States

A   Cancellation marks
    UF Marks, Cancellation
    BT Cancellation
    NT Cancellation slits

A   Cancellation slits
    UF Slits, Cancellation
    BT Cancellation marks

A B Cancelled gatherings
    (Use for gatherings meant to be removed but still present)
    UF Cancellandum gatherings
    BT Cancellation

3

A | B   Cancelled leaves
            (Use for leaves meant to be removed but still present)
            UF Cancellandum leaves
            BT Cancellation

        Cancels
            USE Cancellation

A   Casting off
            BT Composition
            NT Casting off errors >

A   Casting off errors
            UF Errors, Casting off
            BT Casting off
            NT Catchword irregularities
                Crowding
                Excess space
                Signing irregularities
                Type-size change
            RT Multiple printers

A   Catchword irregularities
            UF Irregular catchwords
            BT Casting off errors
                Catchwords

A   Catchword patterns
            BT Catchwords

A   Catchwords
            BT Direction lines
            NT Catchword irregularities
                Catchword patterns

        Chainlines, Turned
            USE Turned chainlines

A | B   Chronograms
            BT Imprint date styles

A | B   Cloth printings
            BT Special materials printings

A | B   Colophons

A   Color printing
            NT Printing in multiple colors >
                Printing in a single color

A | B   Colored paper printings
            BT Special materials printings

        Columniation
            USE Pagination

Columniation errors
    USE Pagination errors

A   Composition
    UF Setting type
       Typesetting
    NT Casting off >
       Justification
       Re-setting
       Setting order >
    RT Composition errors >
       Compositor's copy
       Compositor's setting preferences >
       Multiple printers
       Page make-up >
       Pagination >

A   Composition errors
    (Use for dittography, omissions of text, misspelling, and any
    other compositorial errors)
    UF Errors, Composition
    NT Dittography
       Text omissions
    RT Composition >

A   Compositor's copy
    (Use for the manuscript or book from which the type was set)
    UF Printer's setting copy
    RT Composition >

A   Compositor's setting preferences
    (Use for any evidence of compositorial preference in spelling,
    capitalization, punctuation, justification, etc.)
    UF Compositor's style
    NT Compositor's spelling preferences
    RT Composition >

A   Compositor's spelling preferences
    (Use for any evidence of compositorial spelling preference)
    UF Spelling preferences
    BT Compositor's setting preferences

Compositor's style
    USE Compositor's setting preferences

A B   Copyright notices
    RT Authentication
       Imprimaturs
       Printing privileges

A   Corrected proofs
    BT Proofs

Corrections in press
    USE Press corrections

Corrections, Manuscript
   USE Manuscript corrections

Corrections, Stamped
   Use Stamped corrections

Counterfeits
   USE Forgeries

A   Crowding
   BT Casting off errors

A   Damaged types
   RT Printing order
      Setting order >

Dates of imprint
   USE Imprint date styles

Dates of imprint, False
   USE False imprint dates

Dates of purchase
   USE Purchase dates

Dating styles
   USE Imprint date styles

Deposit copies
   USE Statutory copies

Devices, Printers'
   USE Printers' devices

Devices, Publishers'
   USE Printers' devices

A   Direction lines
   (Use for lines located directly below the text, mostly blank but
   containing catchwords, signatures, and/or press figures)
   NT Catchwords >
      Press figures
      Signatures >

A   Displaced types
   UF Loose type
   BT Locking-up

A   Dittography
   (Use for unintentional repetition of one or more letters, words,
   or lines in type-setting, as "literatature" for literature)
   BT Composition errors

A B   Drawback notices
   RT Tax stamps

	B	**Dummies**
		(Use for models of the type popular in the 19th century for the promotion and solicitation of sales for books, etc.)
		UF Publishers' dummies
		   Salesmen's dummies
		RT Advance copies
		   Book designers' mock-ups

A		**Duodecimo format** UF 12mo format Twelvemo format BT Formats
A		**Eighteenmo format** UF 18mo format Octodecimo format BT Formats
A	B	**Errata lists** NT Integral errata lists Separate errata lists >
		Errata lists, Integral USE Integral errata lists
		Errata lists, Separate USE Separate errata lists
A	B	**Errata slips** BT Separate errata lists
		Errors, Casting off USE Casting off errors
		Errors, Columniation USE Pagination errors
		Errors, Composition USE Composition errors
		Errors, Foliation USE Pagination errors
		Errors, Imposition USE Imposition errors
		Errors, Page make-up USE Page make-up errors
		Errors, Pagination USE Pagination errors
		Errors, Perfecting USE Perfecting errors
		Errors, Registration USE Register errors

A		Excess space BT Casting off errors

A	B	Facsimiles
		    NT Pen facsimiles
		        Photographic facsimiles
		        Type facsimiles
		    RT Fakes
		        False imprints
		        Forgeries
		        Page-for-page reprints
		        Period printings

A	B	Fakes
		    RT Facsimiles >
		        False imprint dates
		        False imprints
		        Forgeries
		        Made-up copies

A	B	False imprint dates
		    UF Dates of imprint, False
		        Imprint dates, False
		    RT Fakes
		        False imprints

A	B	False imprints
		    UF Imprints, False
		    RT Facsimiles >
		        Fakes
		        False imprint dates
		        Fictitious imprints

A	B	Fictitious imprints
		    UF Imprints, Fictitious
		    RT False imprints

A	B	Fine paper printings
		    (Use for items identified as produced on fine paper, often in
		    limited editions)
		    BT Special materials printings

		Foliation USE Pagination
		Foliation errors USE Pagination errors

A		Folio format
		    UF 2o format
		    BT Formats

A B Forgeries
    UF Counterfeits
    RT Authentication
       Facsimiles >
       Fakes
       Piracies

A   Formats
    (Use for imposition formats only including formats not found as
    narrower terms in this thesaurus)
    BT Imposition
    NT Broadsheet format
       Folio format
       Quarto format
       Octavo format
       Duodecimo format
       Sixteenmo format
       Eighteenmo format
       Twenty-fourmo format
       Thirty-twomo format
       Sixty-fourmo format

A   Furniture impressions
    (Use for accidental impressions of furniture)
    UF Impressions, Furniture
    BT Locking-up

A   Galley proofs
    BT Proofs

  B Gratis copies
    RT Advance copies
       Review copies
       Sample copies

Guard sheets, Printed
    USE Printed guard sheets

A   Half-sheet imposition
    UF Work and turn
    BT Imposition

A B Handmade paper printings
    BT Special materials printings

A   Headline irregularities
    UF Running title irregularities
    BT Headline patterns

A   Headline patterns
    UF Running title patterns
    BT Headlines
    NT Headline irregularities

A		**Headlines**
		   UF Running titles
		   NT Headline patterns >
		   RT Skeletons

A		**Imposition**
		   NT Formats >
		      Half-sheet imposition
		      Imposition errors
		      Re-imposition
		      Skeletons
		      Turned chainlines
		      Wraparound gatherings

A		**Imposition errors**
		   UF Errors, Imposition
		   BT Imposition

		Impressions, Bearer USE Bearer impressions
		Impressions, Furniture USE Furniture impressions
		Impressions, Space USE Space impressions
		Impressions, Type-body USE Type-body impressions

A	B	**Imprimaturs**
		   UF Imprimum potest
		      Licenses
		      Nihil obstat
		   RT Copyright notices
		      Printing privileges

		Imprimum potest USE Imprimaturs

A	B	**Imprint date styles**
		   UF Calendar styles
		      Dates of imprint
		      Dating styles
		   NT Chronograms

		Imprint dates, False USE False imprint dates
		Imprints, False USE False imprints
		Imprints, Fictitious USE Fictitious imprints
		In-house manuscript corrections USE Manuscript corrections

```
        In-press corrections
            USE Press corrections

A       Inking
            NT Re-inking
            RT Color printing >

A | B   Inserted text leaves
            (Use for leaves of text inserted within or between uncancelled
            gatherings)
            BT Insertions
            RT Cancel leaves
                Signing irregularities >

A | B   Insertions
            NT Inserted text leaves
                Printed guard sheets
                Separate errata lists
            RT States

A | B   Integral errata lists
            UF Errata lists, Integral
            BT Errata lists

A       Inverted blocks
            UF Blocks, Inverted
            BT Page make-up errors

        Irregular catchwords
            USE Catchword irregularities

        Irregularly shaped books
            USE Shaped books

        Irregularly signed gatherings
            USE Signing irregularities

    B   Issues*
            NT Binding issues
                Re-issues
                Simultaneous issues
            RT Special materials printings >
                States
```

* Determination of "issue" is considerably more complicated than is determination of "state" and these terms must be applied with care. Though exact definitions vary, one can say that "issue" refers to a consciously planned publishing unit whereas "state" is a term which applies to differences (often resulting from an error or attempt to correct an error) among printed sheets of a single impression or issue. Chapters 2 and 11 of Bowers' Principles of Bibliographical Description offer what is probably the most thorough treatment of the two concepts. McKerrow discusses them in less depth in chapter 3, part 2, of his An Introduction to Bibliography. G. Thomas Tanselle provides particularly useful, concise definitions at the end of his article, "The Bibliographical Concepts of 'Issue' and 'State'", in Papers of the Bibliographical Society of America 69 (1975):17-66.

A   Justification
       (Use for any evidence of justification process or lack of it)
       BT Composition

       Label cancels
         USE Cancel slips

       Labels, Booksellers'
         USE Booksellers' labels

A B   Large paper printings
       BT Special materials printings

       Licenses
         USE Imprimaturs
           Printing privileges

   B   Limitation statements
       UF Limited editions
       RT Special materials printing >

       Limited editions
         USE Limitation statements

A   Locking-up
       NT Bearer impressions
          Displaced types
          Furniture impressions
          Pulled types
          Space impressions
          Type-body impressions

       Loose type
         USE Displaced types
           Pulled types
           Space impressions
           Type-body impressions

   B   Made-up copies
       UF Sophisticated copies
       RT Fakes

A B   Manuscript corrections
       (Use for manuscript corrections believed to have been made in the
       printing or publishing house)
       UF Corrections, Manuscript
         In-house manuscript corrections
       RT Cancellation

       Marks, Cancellation
         USE Cancellation marks

A B   Miniature books
       (Use for volumes 10cm or less in height)

```
Mottoes, Printers'
    USE Printers' mottoes

Mottoes, Publishers'
    USE Printers' mottoes

Multiple color printing
    USE Printing in multiple colors
```

A
```
Multiple printers
    (Use for evidence of a book having been set or printed by division
    among different workmen or firms)
    RT Casting off errors >
       Composition >
       Press figures
```

B
```
Multiple publishers
    (Use for evidence of a book having been published by more than one
    publisher, such as title-pages with no difference in setting other
    than the publisher statement)
    RT Simultaneous issues

Nihil obstat
    USE Imprimaturs
```

A
```
Octavo format
    UF 8vo format
    BT Formats

Octodecimo format
    USE Eighteenmo format

Omissions of text
    USE Text omissions
```

A B
```
Page-for-page reprints
    (Use for evidence indicating an item has been set following the
    page make-up of an earlier edition)
    UF Setting by pages
    RT Facsimiles
       Re-setting
```

A
```
Page make-up
    NT Page make-up errors >
    RT Composition >
```

A
```
Page make-up errors
    UF Errors, Page make-up
    BT Page make-up
    NT Inverted blocks
```

A
```
Page proofs
    BT Proofs
```

A | | Pagination
(Use for any evidence of pagination, foliation, or columniation pattern or practice)
UF Columniation
Foliation
NT Pagination errors
RT Composition >

A | | Pagination errors
UF Columniation errors
Errors, Columniation
Errors, Foliation
Errors, Pagination
Foliation errors
BT Pagination

| B | Pen facsimiles
BT Facsimiles

A | | Perfecting
(Use for alignment of text on opposite sides of printed leaf)
UF Backing-up
NT Perfecting errors
RT Register >

A | | Perfecting errors
UF Errors, Perfecting
BT Perfecting

A | B | Period printings
(Use for conscious imitations of earlier printing styles)
RT Facsimiles >

| B | Photographic facsimiles
BT Facsimiles

| B | Piracies
UF Pirated editions
RT Authentication
Forgeries

Pirated editions
USE Piracies

A | | Press corrections
UF Corrections in press
In-press corrections
Running corrections
Stop press corrections
RT Proofs >
Re-imposition
Re-setting
States

A		Press figures
		UF Press numbers
		BT Direction lines
		RT Multiple printers

Press numbers
   USE Press figures

Prices of books
   USE Book prices
      Second-hand prices

A   Printed guard sheets
   UF Guard sheets, Printed
   BT Insertions

Printer's setting copy
   USE Compositor's copy

A B   Printers' devices
   UF Devices, Printers'
      Devices, Publishers'
      Printers' marks
      Publishers' devices

Printers' marks
   USE Printers' devices

A B   Printers' mottoes
   UF Mottoes, Printers'
      Mottoes, Publishers'
      Publishers' mottoes

A   Printing in a single color
   (Use for items printed entirely in a color other than black)
   BT Color printing

A   Printing in multiple colors
   (Use for items printed in more than one color, e.g., red and
   black)
   UF Multiple color printing
   BT Color printing
   NT Printing in multiple colors at one pass
      Printing in multiple colors in separate passes

A   Printing in multiple colors at one pass
   (Use for items with multiple colors in which all colors have
   been printed simultaneously)
   BT Printing in multiple colors

A   Printing in multiple colors in separate passes
   (Use for items with multiple colors in which different colors
   have been printed successively)
   BT Printing in multiple colors

A		Printing order

(Use for evidence of printing order, such as progressively damaged types or distorted rules)
    RT Damaged types
       Setting order >

A	B	Printing privileges

    UF Licenses
       Privileges, Printing
    RT Copyright notices
       Imprimaturs

	B	Private press books

	B	Privately published books

(Use for books published for private distribution only)

Privileges, Printing
    USE Printing privileges

A		Proofs

    NT Corrected proofs
       Galley proofs
       Page proofs
       Uncorrected proofs
    RT Press corrections

Publishers' devices
    USE Printers' devices

Publishers' dummies
    USE Dummies

Publishers' mottoes
    USE Printers' mottoes

Publishers' series
    USE Series

A		Pulled types

    UF Loose type
    BT Locking-up

	B	Purchase dates

(Use for dates of original purchase)
    UF Dates of purchase

A		Quarto format

    UF 4to format
    BT Formats

A		Re-imposition

    BT Imposition
    RT Press corrections

A		Re-inking

    BT Inking

	B	Re-issues
		UF Remainder issues
		BT Issues
		RT Standing type
A		Re-setting
		BT Composition
		RT Page-for-page reprints
		Press corrections
A		Register

Register
(Use for alignment of different colors when printing one side of a sheet in two or more passes through the press, as in red-and-black printing)
NT Register errors
RT Perfecting >

A   Register errors
        UF Errors, Registration
        BT Register

Registers of signatures
    USE Signature registers

Remainder issues
    USE Re-issues

Repeated signatures
    USE Signing repetitions

B   Review copies
        RT Advance copies
            Gratis copies
            Sample copies

Running corrections
    USE Press corrections

Running title irregularities
    USE Headline irregularities

Running title patterns
    USE Headline patterns

Running titles
    USE Headlines

Salesmen's dummies
    USE Dummies

B   Sample copies
        (Use for pre-publication advertisement copies)
        UF Blad
        RT Advance copies
            Gratis copies
            Review copies

	B	Second-hand prices 　　UF Auction prices 　　　　Prices of books 　　RT Book prices
A	B	Separate errata lists 　　UF Errata lists, Separate 　　BT Errata lists 　　　　Insertions 　　NT Errata slips
	B	Series 　　UF Publishers' series
A		Setting by formes 　　(Use for evidence that text has been set by formes, i.e., in the 　　order in which it is imposed upon the press, rather than seriatim) 　　BT Setting order
		Setting by pages 　　USE Page-for-page reprints
A		Setting order 　　BT Composition 　　NT Setting by formes 　　　　Setting seriatim 　　RT Damaged types 　　　　Printing order
A		Setting seriatim 　　(Use for evidence that the text has been set seriatim, i.e., 　　consecutively from beginning to end, rather than by formes) 　　BT Setting order
		Setting type 　　USE Composition
		Sexagesimo-quarto format 　　USE Sixty-fourmo format
		Sexto-decimo format 　　USE Sixteenmo format
A	B	Shaped books 　　(Use for books of other than a conventional rectangular shape, 　　e.gg., circular, triangular, irregularly polygonal books) 　　UF Irregularly shaped books 　　　　Specially shaped books
A		Signature registers 　　(Use for the lists or summaries of signatures often printed at the 　　end of early printed books) 　　UF Registers of signatures 　　RT Signatures

A Signatures
    (Use for the symbols used to distinguish gatherings and put them
    in order)
    BT Direction lines
    NT Signing patterns >
    RT Signature registers

A Signing gaps
    BT Signing irregularities

A Signing irregularities
    UF Irregularly signed gatherings
    BT Casting off errors
       Signing patterns
    NT Signing gaps
       Signing repetitions
       Unsigned gatherings
    RT Inserted text leaves

A Signing patterns
    BT Signatures
    NT Signing irregularities >

A Signing repetitions
    UF Repeated signatures
    BT Signing irregularities

B Simultaneous issues
    (Use for evidence of a book being published in two or more issues
    simultaneously)
    BT Issues
    RT Multiple publishers

A Sixteenmo format
    UF 16mo format
       Sexto-decimo format
    BT Formats

A Sixty-fourmo format
    UF 64mo format
       Sexagesimo-quarto format
    BT Formats

A Skeletons
    BT Imposition
    RT Headlines >

Slip cancels
    USE Cancel slips

Slits, Cancellation
    USE Cancellation slits

Sophisticated copies
    USE Made-up copies

A		Space impressions
		    (Use for accidental impressions of spacing material)
		    UF Accidental type impressions
		       Impressions, Space
		       Loose type
		    BT Locking-up

A	B	Special materials printings
		    (Use for printings or issues of a work that are made, generally in
		    relatively small numbers of copies, on distinctive materials)
		    NT Cloth printings
		       Colored paper printings
		       Fine paper printings
		       Handmade paper printings
		       Large paper printings
		       Vellum printings
		       Wood printings
		    RT Issues
		       Limitation statements

		Specially shaped books USE Shaped books
		Spelling preferences USE Compositor's spelling preferences

A	B	Stamped corrections
		    UF Corrections, Stamped
		    RT Cancellation >

	B	Standing type RT Re-issues

A	B	States*
		    RT Cancellation >
		       Insertions >
		       Issues >
		       Press corrections

	B	Statutory copies UF Deposit copies
		Stop press corrections USE Press corrections
	B	Subscribers' addresses RT Subscription lists
	B	Subscription lists RT Subscribers' addresses

* See note at foot of page 11.

A	B	Tax stamps RT Drawback notices

A		Text omissions
		    (Use for omission of a word or words from intended text as a
		    result of composition error)
		    UF Omissions of text
		    BT Composition errors

A		Thirty-twomo format
		    UF 32mo format
		       Tricesimo-secundo format
		    BT Formats

		Tricesimo-secundo format USE Thirty-twomo format

A		Turned chainlines
		    UF Chainlines, Turned
		    BT Imposition

		Twelvemo format USE Duodecimo format

A		Twenty-fourmo format
		    UF 24mo format
		       Vicesimo-quarto format
		    BT Formats

A	B	Type facsimiles BT Facsimiles

A		Type-body impressions
		    (Use for accidental impressions of pieces of type, showing type
		    height)
		    UF Accidental type impressions
		       Impressions, Type-body
		       Loose type
		    BT Locking-up

A		Type-size change BT Casting off errors
		Typesetting USE Composition
A		Uncorrected proofs BT Proofs
A		Unsigned gatherings BT Signing irregularities
A	B	Vellum printings BT Special materials printings

Vicesimo-quarto format
USE Twenty-fourmo format

A B Wood printings
(Use for items printed on wood)
BT Special materials printings

Work and turn
USE Half-sheet imposition

A Wraparound gatherings
(Use for sheets on which non-sequential portions of the text, usual-
ly preliminary and final matter, have been printed and then so
folded and assembled with other sheets that part of the gathering
wraps round other gatherings of the item)
BT Imposition

Xylographica
USE Block books

II: Hierarchical list

The arrangement of terms in this list is by broad functional classification, with subclassifications within larger categories. A term which is applicable to more than one general category may occur in each. Certain terms (shown within square brackets [ ]) have been supplied only as explanatory or gathering terms and are not authorized for use in MARC field 755; all other terms in this list are direct entry terms which will be found also in the alphabetical list (section I).

IIA: Hierarchical arrangement of printing terms

Use these terms to retrieve examples of physical evidence of production methods from setting through completion of printing. For evidence relating to publishing and/or bookselling practices, see IIB: Hierarchical arrangement of publishing and bookselling terms.

[Additions and corrections to text]
  Cancellation
    Cancel gatherings
    Cancel leaves
    Cancel slips
    Cancellation marks
      Cancellation slits
    Cancelled gatherings
    Cancelled leaves
    Manuscript corrections
    Stamped corrections
  Errata lists
    Integral errata lists
    Separate errata lists
      Errata slips
  Insertions
    Inserted text leaves
    Printed guard sheets
    Separate errata lists
      Errata slips
  Press corrections
    Re-imposition
    Re-setting
  Proofs
    Corrected proofs
    Galley proofs
    Page proofs
    Uncorrected proofs
  States

[Compositor's work]
   Composition
      Casting off
         Casting off errors
            Catchword irregularities
            Crowding
            Excess space
            Signing irregularities
               Signing gaps
               Signing repetitions
               Unsigned gatherings
            Type-size change
      Composition errors
         Dittography
         Text omissions
      Compositor's copy
      Compositor's setting preferences
         Compositor's spelling preferences
      Direction lines
         Catchwords
            Catchword irregularities
            Catchword patterns
         Press figures
         Signatures
            Signing patterns
               Signing irregularities
                  Signing gaps
                  Signing repetitions
                  Unsigned gatherings
      Headlines
         Headline patterns
            Headline irregularities
      Justification
      Page-for-page reprints
      Page make-up
         Page make-up errors
            Inverted blocks
      Pagination
         Pagination errors
      Re-setting
      Setting order
         [Evidence]
            Damaged types
         Setting by formes
         Setting seriatim
   Imposition
      Formats
         Broadsheet format
         Folio format
         Quarto format
         Octavo format
         Duodecimo format
         Sixteenmo format
         Eighteenmo format
         Twenty-fourmo format
         Thirty-twomo format
         Sixty-fourmo format

[Compositor's work] (continued)

    Half-sheet imposition
    Imposition errors
    [Paper evidence]
      Turned chainlines
    Re-imposition
    Skeletons
      Headlines
        Headline patterns
          Headline irregularities
    Wraparound gatherings

[Control of printing]
    [Copyright and licensing]
      Copyright notices
      Imprimaturs
      Printing privileges
    [Taxes and levies]
      Drawback notices
      Tax stamps

[Dates]
    False imprint dates
    Imprint date styles
      Chronograms

[Fakery, falsification, imitation, and copying]
    Facsimiles
      Type facsimiles
    Fakes
    False imprint dates
    False imprints
    Fictitious imprints
    Forgeries
    Page-for-page reprints
    Period printings

Multiple printers
    Casting off errors
    Composition
    Press figures

[Pressman's work]
    Color printing
      Printing in a single color
      Printing in multiple colors
        Printing in multiple colors at one pass
        Printing in multiple colors in separate passes
    Inking
      Re-inking

[Pressman's work] (continued)

  [Make-ready]
    Locking-up
      [Accidental impressions]
        Bearer impressions
        Furniture impressions
        Space impressions
        Type-body impressions
      Displaced types
      Pulled types
    Perfecting
      Perfecting errors
    Press figures
    Register
      Register errors
  Press corrections
    Re-imposition
    Re-setting
    States
  Printing order
    [Evidence]
      Damaged types

[Printer identification]
  Colophons
  Printers' devices
  Printers' mottoes

Signatures
  Signature registers
  Signing patterns
    Signing irregularities
      Signing gaps
      Signing repetitions
      Unsigned gatherings

[Special shapes, sizes and kinds of books]
  Block books
  Miniature books
  Shaped books
  Special materials printings
    Cloth printings
    Colored paper printings
    Fine paper printings
    Handmade paper printings
    Large paper printings
    Vellum printings
    Wood printings

IIB: Hierarchical arrangement of publishing and bookselling terms
        Use these terms to retrieve examples of physical evidence of publishing
and/or bookselling practices. For evidence relating to printing house proce-
dures and practices, see IIA: Hierarchical arrangement of printing terms.

[Control of publishing]
    [Copyright and licensing]
        Copyright notices
        Imprimaturs
        Printing privileges
        Statutory copies
    [Taxes and levies]
        Drawback notices
        Tax stamps

[Dates]
    False imprint dates
    Imprint date styles
        Chronograms
    Purchase dates

[Distribution and sales methods]
    Booksellers' labels
    Dummies
    Multiple publishers
    [Prices]
        Book prices
        Second-hand prices
    Privately published books
    Series
    Subscribers' addresses
    Subscription lists

[Editions, issues and states]
    Cancellation
        Cancel gatherings
        Cancel leaves
        Cancel slips
        Cancelled gatherings
        Cancelled leaves
        Manuscript corrections
        Stamped corrections
    Errata lists
        Integral errata lists
        Separate errata lists
            Errata slips
    Insertions
        Inserted text leaves
        Separate errata lists
            Errata slips
    Issues
        Binding issues
        Re-issues
            Standing type
        Simultaneous issues
        Special materials printings
            Cloth printings

[Editions, issues and states] (continued)

        Colored paper printings
        Fine paper printings
        Handmade paper printings
        Large paper printings
        Vellum printings
        Wood printings
    Limitation statements
    Multiple publishers
    Piracies
    Privately published books
    States

[Fakery, falsification, imitation, and copying]
    Authentication
    Facsimiles
        Pen facsimiles
        Photographic facsimiles
        Type facsimiles
    Fakes
    False imprint dates
    False imprints
    Fictitious imprints
    Forgeries
    Made-up copies
    Page-for-page reprints
    Period printings
    Piracies

[Publisher identification]
    Colophons
    Printers' devices
    Printers' mottoes

[Special shapes, sizes and kinds of books]
    Block books
    Miniature books
    Private press books
    Shaped books
    Special materials printings
        Cloth printings
        Colored paper printings
        Fine paper printings
        Handmade paper printings
        Large paper printings
        Vellum printings
        Wood printings

[Special use copies]
    Advance copies
    Book designers' mock-ups
    Dummies
    Gratis copies
    Review copies
    Sample copies
    Statutory copies